Everyone Contributes

MAYA LIN

Honoring Our Forgotten Heroes

Bob Italia

Published by Abdo & Daughters, 6535 Cecilia Circle, Edina, Minnesota 55439.

Library bound edition distributed by Rockbottom Books, Pentagon Tower, P.O. Box 36036, Minneapolis, Minnesota 55435.

Edited by Rosemary Wallner

Photo Credits: Archive - pgs. 16, 23
                 Bettmann - pgs. 11, 14
                 Black Star - pgs. 8, 18, 19, 30
                 Wide World - pgs. 5, 27
Cover Photo: Black Star

Library of Congress Cataloging-in-Publication Data

Italia, Robert, 1955-
      Maya Lin: Honoring our Forgotten Heroes/written by Bob Italia.
           p.   cm. -- (Everyone Contributes)
      Summary:Presents the life of the young architect-sculptor who designed the controversial memorial honoring United States soldiers who served in the Vietnam War.
      Includes glossary and index.
      ISBN 1-56239-234-4
      1. Lin, Maya Ying--Criticism and interpretation --Juvenile literature.
2. Vietnam Veterans Memorial (Wash. D.C.)- Juvenile literature.
[1. Lin, Maya Ying.   2. Architects.   3. Sculptors.   4.Vietnam Veterans Memorial (Wash. D.C.)]   I. Title.   II. Series: Italia, Robert, 1955-
Everyone Contributes.
      NA9330.U62W34   1993
      720'.92--dc20
      [B]
                                                          93-10257
                                                             CIP
                                                              AC

Table of Contents

The Monument Maker

Architect and sculptor Maya Lin stands only 5 feet 3 inches tall. But when it comes to monument-making, Lin is a giant among designers.

Lin has built some of the most famous monuments in the United States. She designed the Civil Rights Memorial and the Vietnam Veterans Memorial.

Lin's simple designs are not overwhelming. Like her, they do not tower over people or intimidate them. Instead, they make people pause and reflect. They also draw out emotions.

Sometimes, Lin's designs go even further. The Vietnam Memorial, her greatest work, moved an entire country from anger and confusion about a war to tears. But most importantly, the memorial helped the country remember and honor its forgotten heroes. It also helped the country overcome its grief.

Maya Lin, the designer of the
Vietnam Veterans Memorial.

Maya Lin's Foundation

Maya Ying Lin was born in 1960 in Athens, Ohio. Her parents were professors at Ohio University. Her father, Henry, was dean of fine arts. Her mother, Julia, taught English and Oriental literature. Her older brother, Tan Lin, is a poet at Columbia University.

The Lin family name means "forest." Maya's middle name, Ying (pronounced "ING") means "precious stone." Maya is the name of a Hindu goddess.

Lin's parents immigrated to the United States from China in 1948. Her father had been an academic administrator in China. He had also worked with ceramics. Lin's mother was smuggled out of Shanghai just as the Communists were bombing the city. She escaped with a one hundred dollar bill pinned to her coat lining.

Lin credits her upbringing and Asian roots for her approach to design work.

"My parents very much brought us up to decide what we wanted to do, and when we wanted to study," she said. "There was very little discipline. And yet I don't think we ever did anything that was irresponsible.

"Maybe that is an Eastern philosophy—that you don't force an opinion on a child," she added. "You allow them to draw their own conclusions."

The Yale Experience

Lin attended Yale University in New Haven, Connecticut. There, she studied architecture and sculpture. Her professors wanted her to choose one or the other. Focusing on one subject was the correct way, they said.

"I would look at my professors, smile, and go about my business," she said. "I consider myself both an artist and an architect. I don't combine them, but each field informs the other.

"Architecture, you can say, is like writing a book," she continued. "Everything in a building matters, from the doorknobs to the paint details. And sculpture is like

Maya Lin attended Yale University.
There, she studied architecture and sculpture.

writing a poem. You're not saying as much. It's an idea stripped bare."

Lin uses the ideas she has learned as a sculptor when she designs. Instead of drawing her plans for a building on paper, Lin makes a simple sculpture. She usually uses cardboard or wood for her first rough model.

After she forms the models, Lin makes detailed drawings on paper. Then a more complex design emerges. She produces a second model with a second set of drawings. She presents this second set of drawings to her client for approval. Finally, she makes a detailed set of presentation models and drawings to scale (the correct proportions).

Once her client approves the design, Lin figures out all the little construction details. She thinks about what type of material to use inside the building. She decides the width and height of each step in the stairways.

"You're really figuring out all the dimensions you need to know to get something built," Lin said.

The Wall

Lin was a Yale University senior when she won an open competition to design the national Vietnam Veterans Memorial. It would be located at the Constitutional Gardens in Washington, D.C. She beat out 1,420 other entrants in the much-publicized design competition.

Her winning entry was a series of pastel sketches. It took two weeks to draw after months of study. She walked around the Mall and Constitution Gardens, and studied every detail.

Lin designed two black granite walls joined at the center in a 130-degree angle. The names of the known 58,175 soldiers who died in the war would be inscribed in the wall.

Lin's idea for the Vietnam Memorial came out of a senior-year workshop at Yale on funereal architecture.

"We did designs, from a gateway to a cemetery to a memorial for World War III," Lin said. "We saw this poster about the Vietnam memorial and thought it would be a great way to end the class.

Maya Lin won the competition to design the
Vietnam Veterans Memorial. In this photo she
is holding a model of the memorial.

Lin knew that the relatives of the dead soldiers had gone through a difficult time. How are all these people going to overcome the pain of losing someone? How do you really overcome death? Lin asked herself. That's when she decided to include the names of the men and women who had died. She knew that all Americans should never forget the war.

"If you just keep pretending that nothing happened [in Vietnam]," she said, "if you didn't really accept that death or time or trouble, then you'd never get over it. The only way you can work with history and the only way you can overcome anything is to accept it very, very honestly."

A Controversial Design

Lin won the contest. In the spring of 1981, her design was introduced to the public. Immediately, the design sparked a controversy that threatened its very existence.

Many people did not like "The Wall," as it became known among Vietnam veterans. The *Chicago Tribune* called it "bizarre." The *National Review* called the memorial "a perpetual disgrace." And a *New York Times* article said the memorial was "a black gash of shame."

Despite the controversy, Lin stood by her design. So did Jan Scruggs. He was the Vietnam veteran whose lobbying efforts brought the memorial into being. He had this to say about Lin: "She has an artistic temperament, and she really stood by her guns to make sure that this memorial design was not tampered with. And it was very important that she did that, because throughout the entire controversy that surrounded the memorial, she really believed in this design. She really knew it was going to work. . . .The strength of her own convictions carried us through quite a few conflicts."

People in Washington, D.C., posed the biggest threat. Interior Secretary James Watt denied a much-needed construction permit. Texas financier H. Ross Perot and Senator Jeremiah A. Denton, Jr., also opposed the design.

Many powerful people were opposed to Maya Lin's design. Texas billionaire H. Ross Perot was one of those people who spoke out against the design.

"There were some very powerful people in Washington who were trying to stop this memorial from being built," Scruggs recalled. "They were saying, 'Why are all the other [monuments] white and this is black?' They called it a scar."

Lin took the criticism in stride. "The whole controversy surrounding the Vietnam memorial," she said, "was artist wants her way, artist who didn't go to this war, who's female, who was too young to have served, wants her way. What they didn't understand is you have to let go of it. It's not just for us. That's what makes it public. It never was just for us."

Then Frederick Hart jumped into the fight. Hart was also a sculptor. His design, "The Three Servicemen Statue," was a traditional, oversized statue of three soldiers. He started a campaign that criticized Lin's design. Then he called for the installment of his own sculpture.

A compromise was reached. Both designs were built. The Vietnam Veterans Memorial Fund paid Hart $200,000 for his design. For winning the original contest, Lin received $20,000.

Frederick Hart designed "The Three Servicemen Statue." He wanted his design for the memorial. He started a campaign that criticized Lin's design.

Turning Anger into Grief

The Wall was finally built. Overnight, public attitude changed. Suddenly, the nation had a memorial it could see and touch. Suddenly, all the known casualties of the war were there, together, in one special place, facing us. They were gone—but not forgotten.

The memorial forced Americans to deal with the pent-up emotions about the war. It eased anger. But most of all, it invited everyone to grieve for the fallen heroes.

"This one superb design has changed the way war memorials—and monuments as a whole—are perceived," said the judges. They approved a 1988 Presidential Design Award for Lin's creation.

People came to the memorial to see the names of their fallen loved ones. Some even scratched the names onto pieces of paper to take home with them. This activity has now turned into a national tradition. Today, the Wall is the most visited memorial in the United States.

The memorial helped Americans ease their
anger. It invited everyone to grieve
for the fallen heroes.

After the Wall was built, the nation had a
memorial it could see and touch. Finally, all
the casualties were together in one place.

Lin's design came from a personal desire. She wanted to create a monument that was not imposing. She wanted her creation to draw emotions from viewers. She did not want the monument to overwhelm them.

"My instinct was to try not to overpower the site with Man's mark," she said. "If I build something in the landscape, the two create a dialogue. It's not like you place the castle on top of the hill.

"In Washington, you had an incredible existing condition," she added. "The way the Lincoln Memorial is situated on one side of the reflecting pool is in dialogue with the Washington Monument. So now you're adding a third party. How do you do that? You don't want this object out there trying to scream for attention—'Me, too! Me, too!' That's one of the reasons why the Vietnam Wall points to both memorials. It includes them."

There was purpose to the Wall, Lin said. It was "to help the veterans coming back, to help their families, to talk to people 100 years from now who will know nothing about that war and nobody on that wall.

To me, it's a very simple notion: You cannot ever forget that war is not just a victory or loss. It's really about individual lives."

The Civil Rights Memorial

After the Wall, Lin made a promise not do any more memorials. But in 1987, the Southern Poverty Law Center (SPLC) in Montgomery, Alabama, pulled her out of early retirement.

"We phoned every Lin in the New York phone books," recalled Morris Dees, the group's executive director.

Dees wanted Lin to build a monument to the people involved in the civil rights movement. Montgomery was the perfect site. That is where the 1955-1956 bus boycott began the civil rights movement. The protest also launched the career of Dr. Martin Luther King, Jr.

Lin was surprised that a civil rights memorial hadn't already been built. She felt compelled to take the assignment.

To begin the project, Lin studied books about the civil rights movement. She wanted to find an emotional link with the turbulent and dramatic events of the 1950s and 1960s.

"Before I even think about form," she said, "I tend to think about all the conceptual, psychological, and intellectual abstracts of what I'm doing. . .I read through a lot of the history. . .I chased down every single little fact.

"The one [fact] that really shocked me was Samuel Younge Jr.'s death," she continued. "I should have remembered that about the time I was entering grade school someone was killed for refusing to use a 'coloreds-only' restroom. I don't think it was ever taught. That's what alarmed me, how quickly this part of our history has been forgotten."

Then Lin found the answer to her design problem. It was contained in Martin Luther King Jr.'s famous speech at the 1963 march on Washington.

One line caught her attention. It read, "With this faith we will be able to hew out of the mountain of despair a stone of hope."

*Martin Luther King Jr.'s famous speech
at the 1963 march on Washington.*

It told Lin she must use the dark granite that she made famous with the Vietnam Memorial. Then another line gave her more vision.

"I had read through Dr. Martin Luther King's 'I Have a Dream' speech once," she recalled, "and I read it through again. I got caught on one line: 'We are not satisfied, and we will not be satisfied until justice rolls down like waters and righteousness like a mighty stream.'

"Something clicked," she continued. "I wanted to work with water, and I wanted again to use words, because that's sort of the clearest, most succinct way to remember history—more so than an image, at times."

The memorial was to be at ground level in front of the SPLC building. Lin's main challenge was to make the memorial fit in with the existing structure, not overwhelm it.

"The building was dead symmetrical," Lin said, "with two staircases on either side leading to a center staircase that led into the building. It funnelled you in. There was very little breathing space. So that was something I wanted to address: to create a sense of arrival."

Lin replaced the two staircases with one slightly curving staircase on the right side. She placed the memorial's shallow reflecting pool at the left edge of the portico. The inspirational King quote was etched on a black granite wall. A thin sheet of water cascades over it and into the pool.

Lin also placed a circular black granite water table in front of the granite wall. The table is inscribed with a chronology of the civil rights movement from May 17, 1954, to April 4, 1968. (On May 17, 1954, the Supreme Court struck down school segregation in *Brown v. Board of Education of Topeka*. On April 4, 1968, Dr. Martin Luther King , Jr., was assassinated.)

"It's really based on the idea that everything doesn't have to look the same to be balanced," Lin said. "And that is something I think is very much part of the conceptual design of the Civil Rights Memorial."

Lin chose black granite because it is the most reflective type of stone. She wanted visitors to be able to see themselves as they read the words.

"The Civil Rights Memorial is about sensitizing the person," she added. "The quality of the water, being able to put your hand on the words under the water, being able to see yourself reflected in it, the fact that you will hear a very quiet water movement—everything adds up to how you will experience the piece."

While she worked on the Civil Rights Memorial, Lin received a grant in 1988 from the National Endowment for the Arts. The money she received breathed new life into her sculpturing career.

In October 1989, Lin finished an open-air peace chapel at Juniata College in Huntingdon, Pennsylvania. She also began restoring a Norwich, Connecticut, mansion. Then on November 5, 1989, Lin's Civil Rights Memorial was finally dedicated.

After her work was finished, Lin returned to her apartment in lower Manhattan, New York. She wanted to be out of the national spotlight.

"I go through stages where I do a project and I'm in the public eye," she said. "And then I duck out and concentrate on my work.

Maya Lin concentrating on her work.
Here she is working on the restoration of a
Norwich, Connecticut mansion.

"I've been incredibly fortunate to have been given the opportunity to work on not just one but both memorials," Lin continued. "They are special. They mark the beginning and closing of a decade."

In the six months following the SPLC dedication, Lin received ten sculpture and architect projects. One was the creation of a landscape park in Charlotte, North Carolina. Another was a sculpture piece commemorating the 20th anniversary of "Women at Yale."

For the Yale project, Lin designed another granite piece and called it the "Women's Table." A polished stone tabletop was cut from green granite in the shape of an oval. Water gently flows over the top of the table.

The table is mounted on a 69-degree angle which commemorates the year 1969. That was the first year women were allowed at Yale. After years of work, the sculpture was finally dedicated in May 1992.

Lin continues to pursue her architectural and sculpting passions. She spends most of her time working in her huge loft apartment in New York City. One end of the room contains her architectural office and drafting studio. At the other end sits her living area and a workshop.

Lin's sculptures run from $6,000 to $12,000 each. They take one or two years to complete—and usually sell right away.

Maya Lin's Legacy

Maya Lin is still young. When the "Women's Table" was complete, she was still in her early thirties. But already she has left her mark. Not only has she contributed to America's well-being, but her works have also honored others who have contributed.

Future generations will stand before her most famous creations. Like us, they will ponder and reflect, and feel the pain of our loss. But most importantly, they will remember our fallen heroes. And that's just what Maya Lin had in mind.

Maya Lin is in her early thirties and feels that she has much more to contribute. But already she has left her mark on us and many generations to come.

GLOSSARY

Architect—A person who designs buildings and supervises their construction.

Boycott—To abstain from using or buying a product or dealing with a company as a means of protest or coercion.

Chronology—The science of measuring time and of dating events.

Granite—A hard, igneous rock composed chiefly of quartz, felspar, and mica.

Immigrant—One who comes into a country to settle there.

Landscape—An expanse of natural scenery seen in one view.

Monument—A building, statue, or other object built to honor a person or event.

Portico—A porch or covered walk consisting of a roof supported by columns.

Professor—A college teacher of the highest rank.

Sculptor—An artist who creates figures in stone, clay, or any other material.

Symmetrical—A balanced or harmonious arrangement or construction.

INDEX